School Skills

This book belongs to
Jenna

Compare

Color the largest picture in each row.

Time to Trace

Trace each line from the bee to the flower.

Twins

Color the two pictures that are alike in each row.

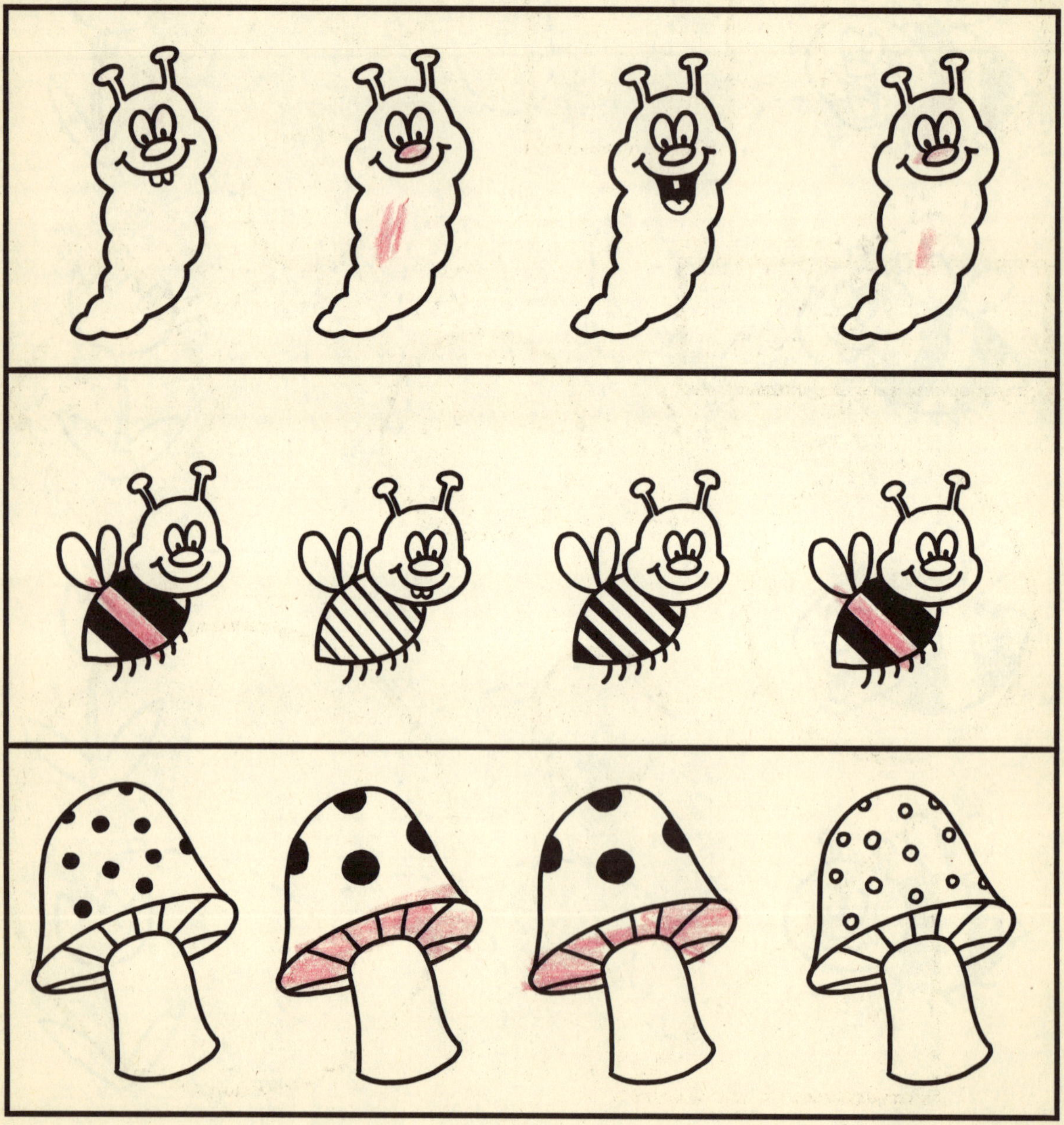

Round Shapes

Color all the circles.

Four Corners

Color all the rectangles.

Three Corners

Color all the triangles.

A Special Kind of Rectangle

Color all the squares.

Funny Faces

In each row, make the faces look like the first one.

Matching

Draw lines between the matching bears.

Matching Pictures

Draw lines between the matching pictures.

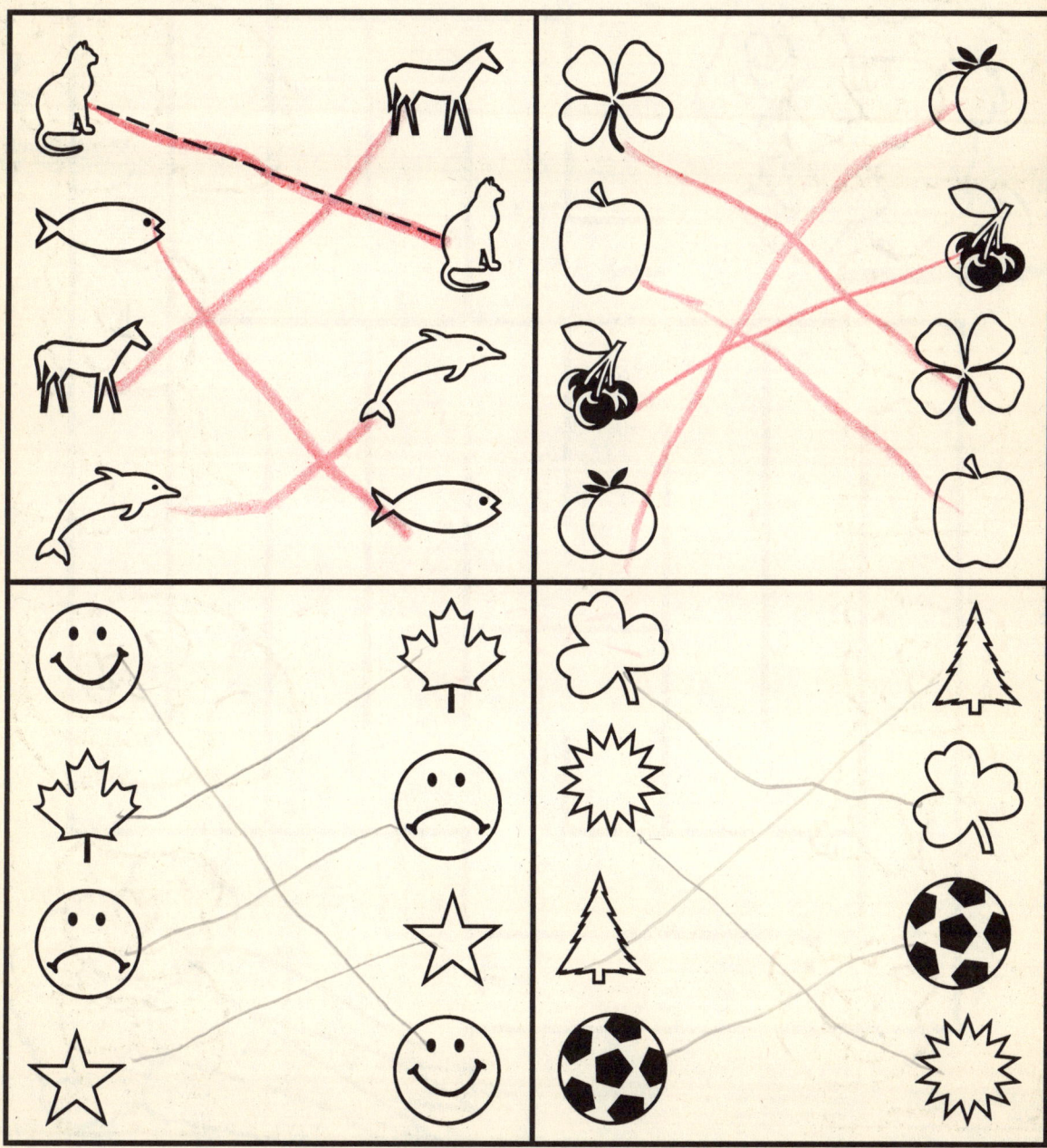

Follow the Maze

Help Bunny find the carrots.

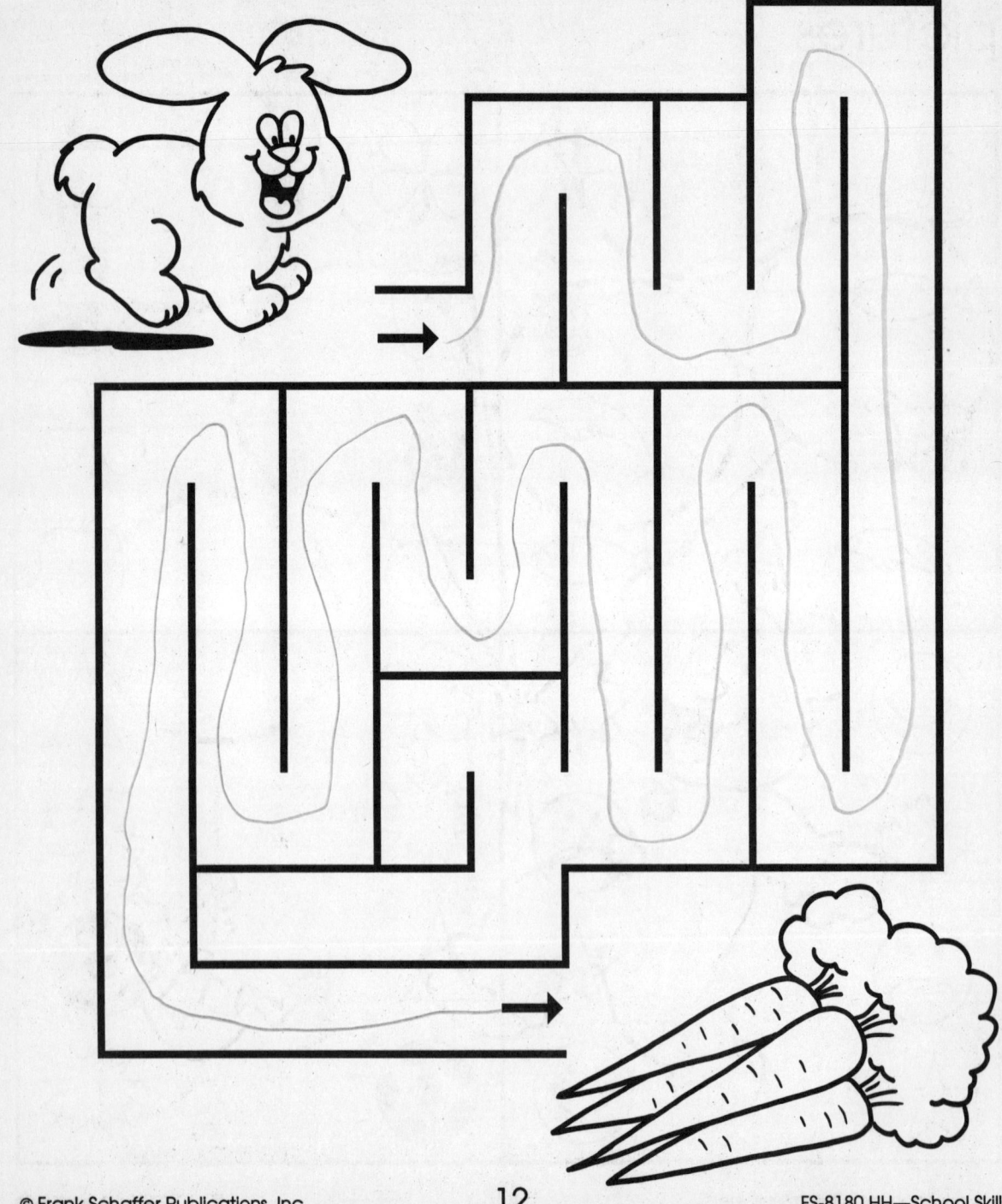

Balloons!

Trace the balloons. Color the picture.

Dot-to-Dot

Connect the dots from 1 to 10.

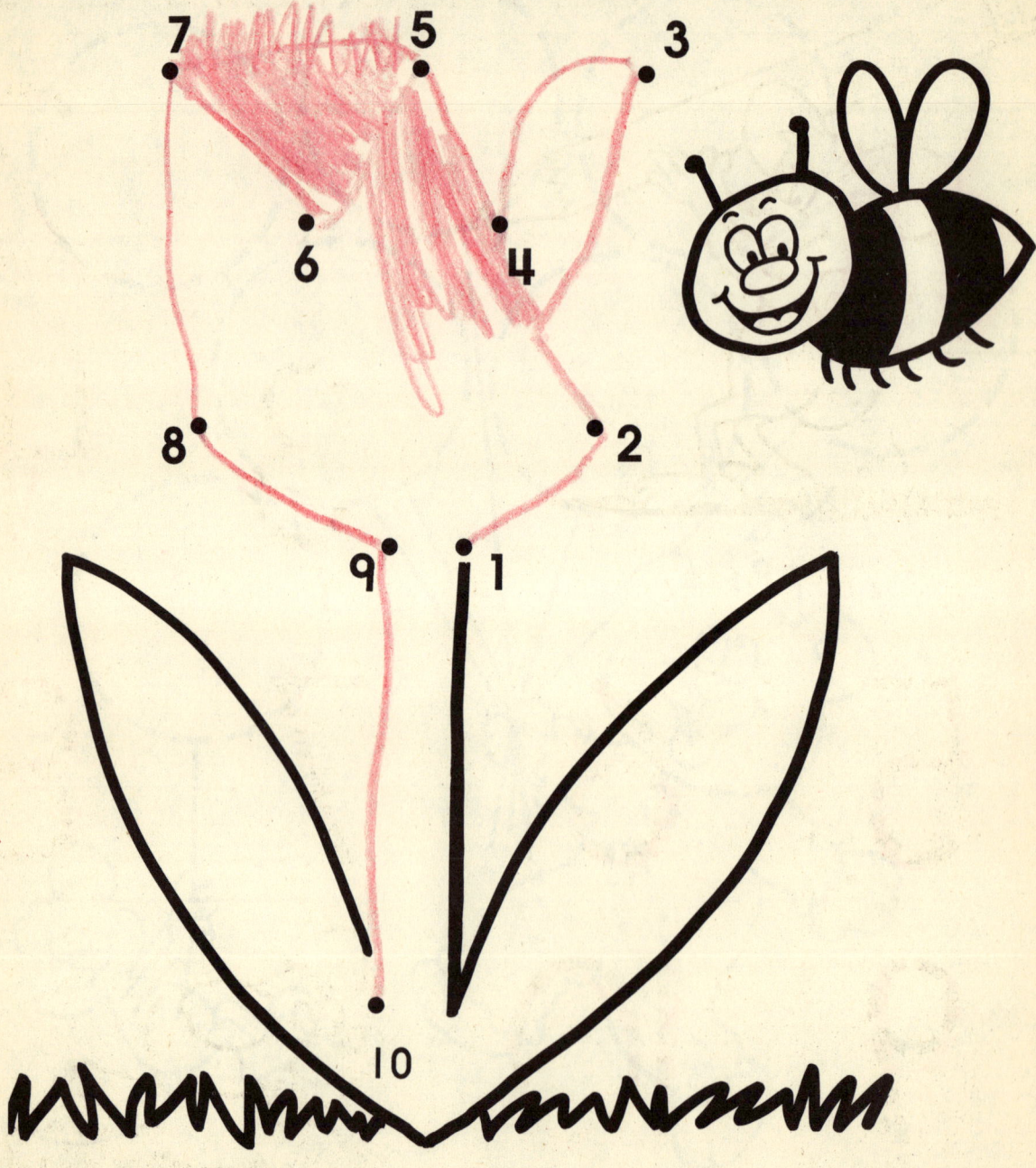

Count Them

Circle the correct number in each box.

2   ⓷

②   3

3   ④

③   4

Draw Carefully

Trace the shapes in each row.

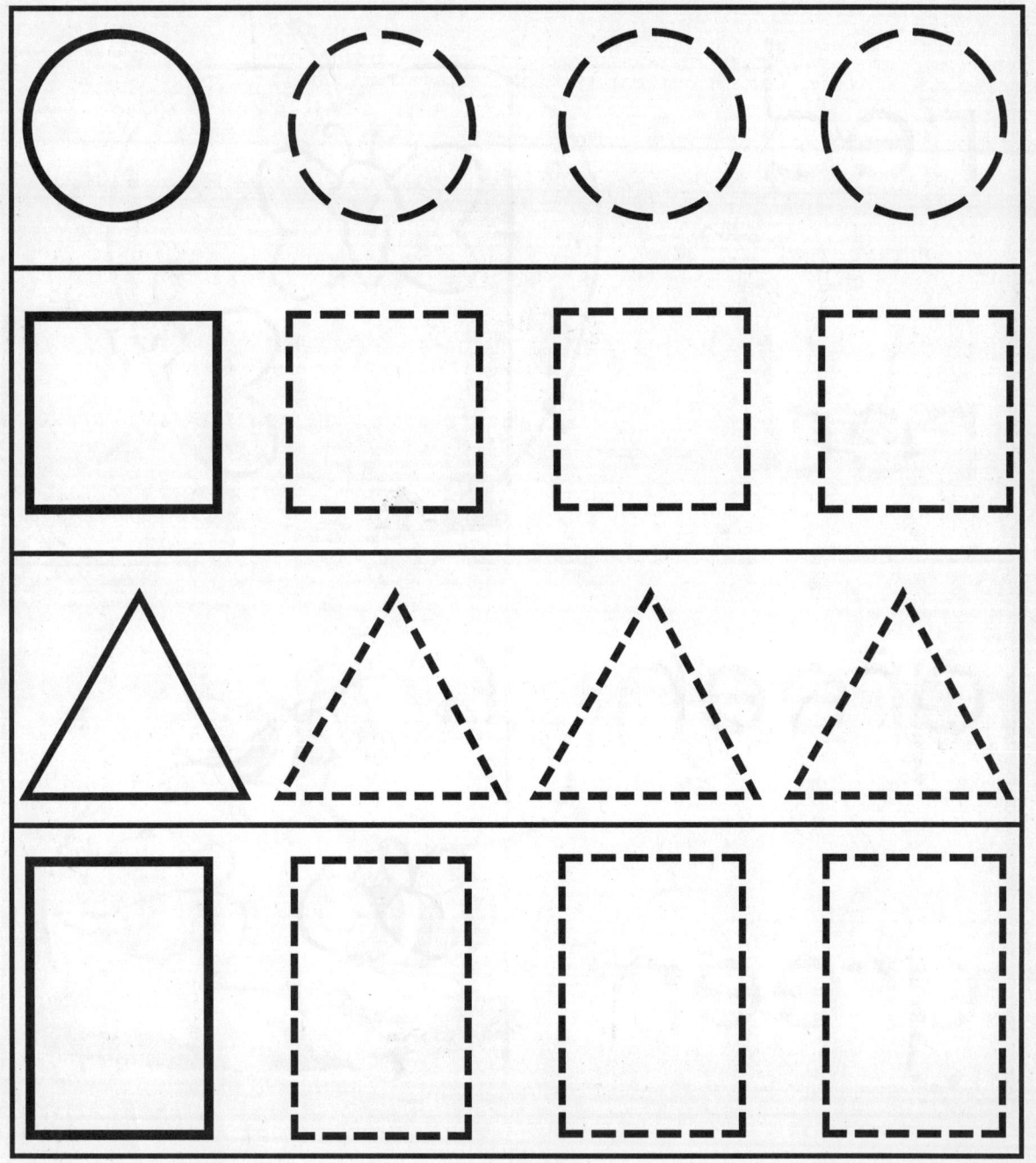

Colors

Trace the word and color the picture.

Do You Know These Colors?

Trace the word and color the picture.

Say the Color

Trace the word and color the picture.

More Colors!

Trace the word and color the picture.

Daisies

Draw a happy flower.

Look Carefully

Circle the matching letters in each row.

a	a	b	a	g	d	a
n	n	m	n	n	r	n
p	p	a	d	b	p	p
z	z	z	x	v	z	y

The Lowercase Alphabet

Trace each letter and say its name.

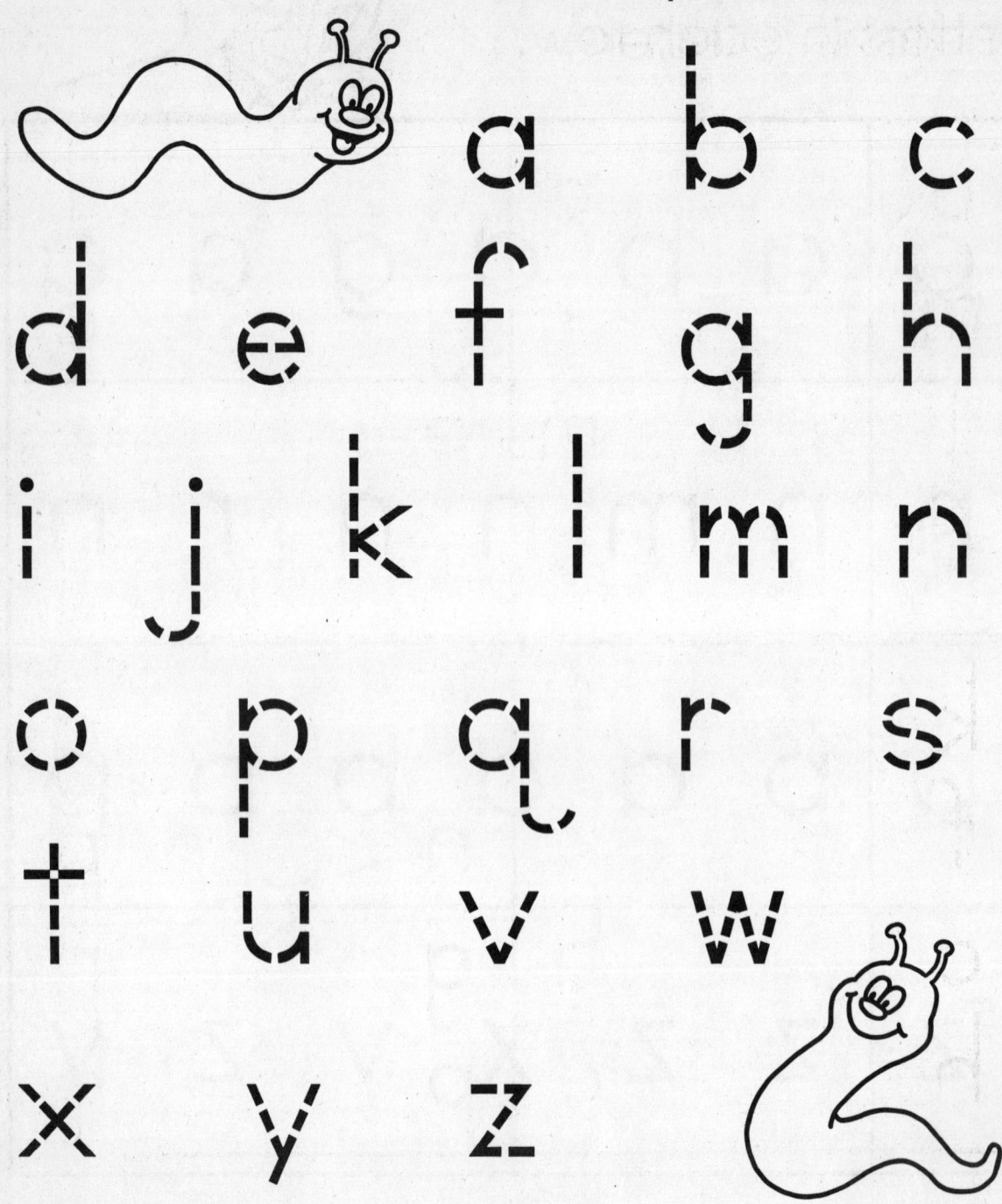

More Lowercase Letters

Draw lines between the matching letters.

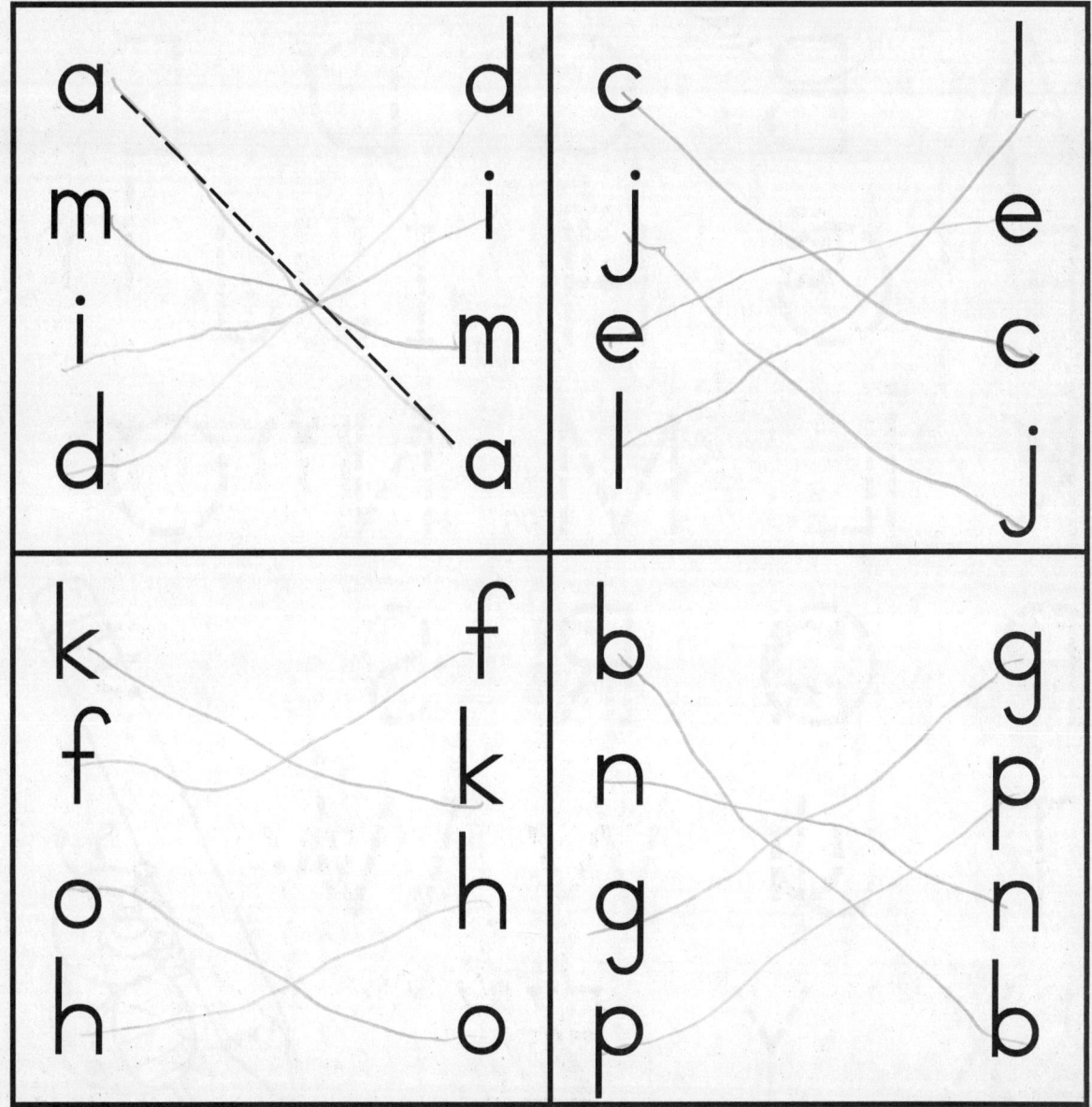

The Uppercase Alphabet

Trace each letter and say its name.

A B C D E

F G H I J

K L M N O

P Q R S

T U V W

X Y Z

Match the Letters

Draw lines between the letters that have the same name.

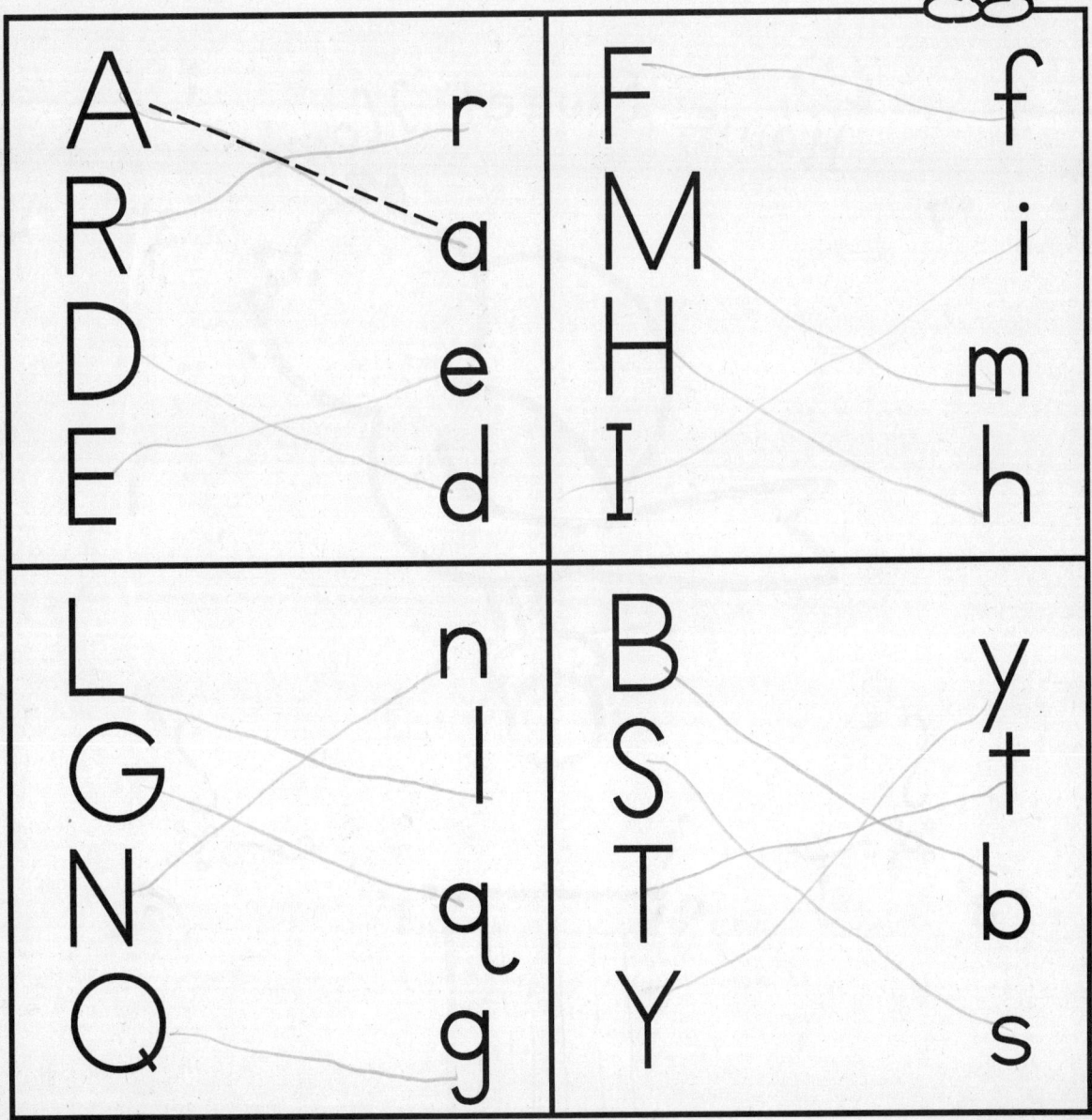

What Is It?

Connect the dots from 1 to 10.

Count and Color

Color 1.

Color 2.

Color 3.

Writing Numbers

Trace and write the numbers.

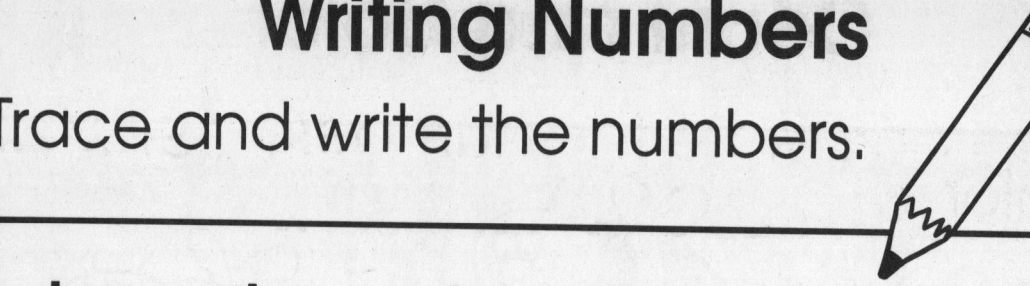

1	1	1
2	2	2
3	3	3
4	4	4
5	5	5

More Numbers

Trace and write the numbers.

6	6	6	
7	7	7	
8	8	8	
9	9	9	
10	10	10	

Study the Shapes

Copy each shape carefully.

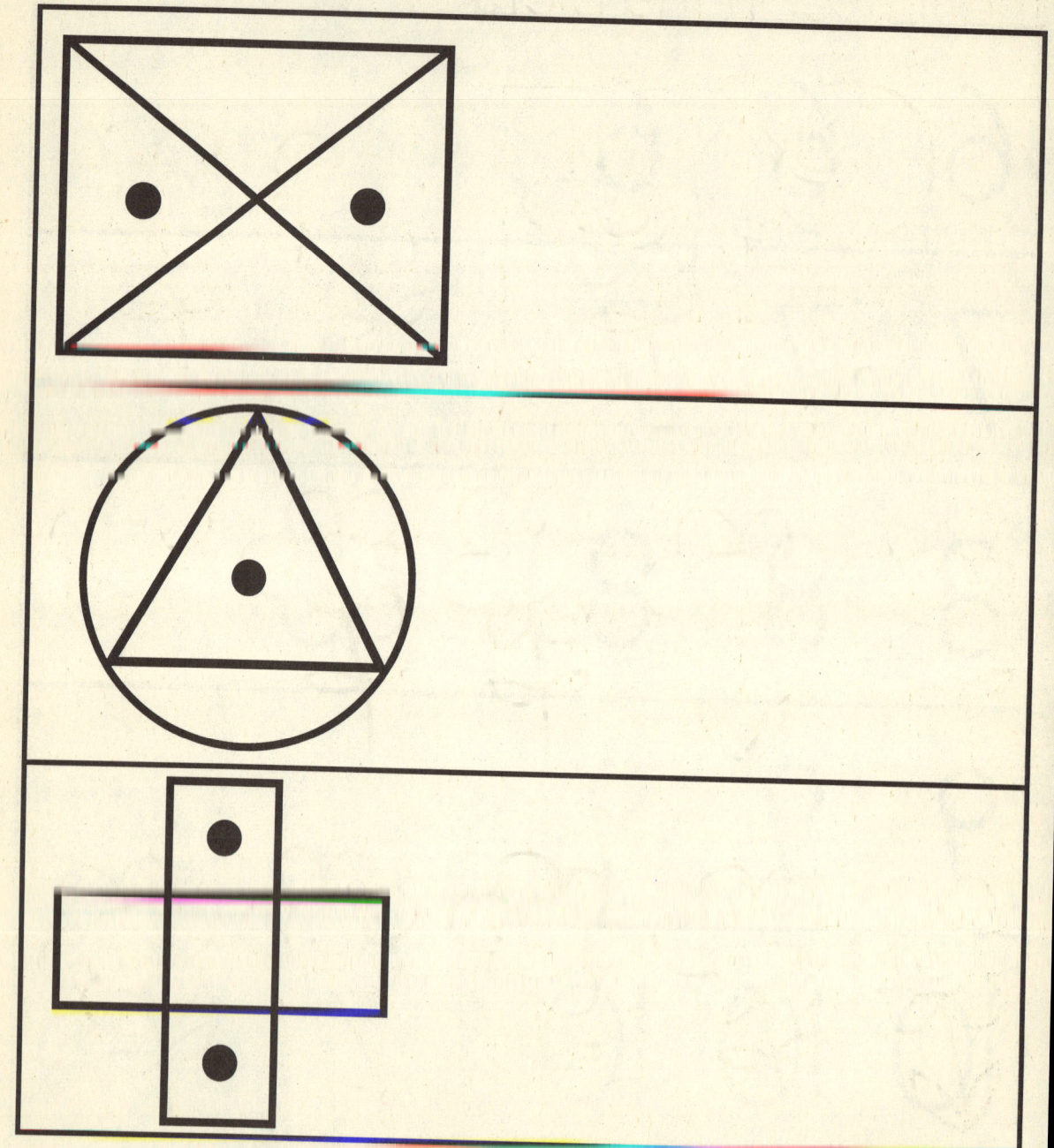

Lowercase Letters

Connect the dots from **a** to **z**.

Count and Color

Monkey Business

Help the monkey find 6 .

Find the Little One

Color the smallest picture in each row.

Clowning Around

Finish the picture of Clara the Clown. Make both sides exactly the same!

Hippity Hop

Connect the dots from **a** to **z**.

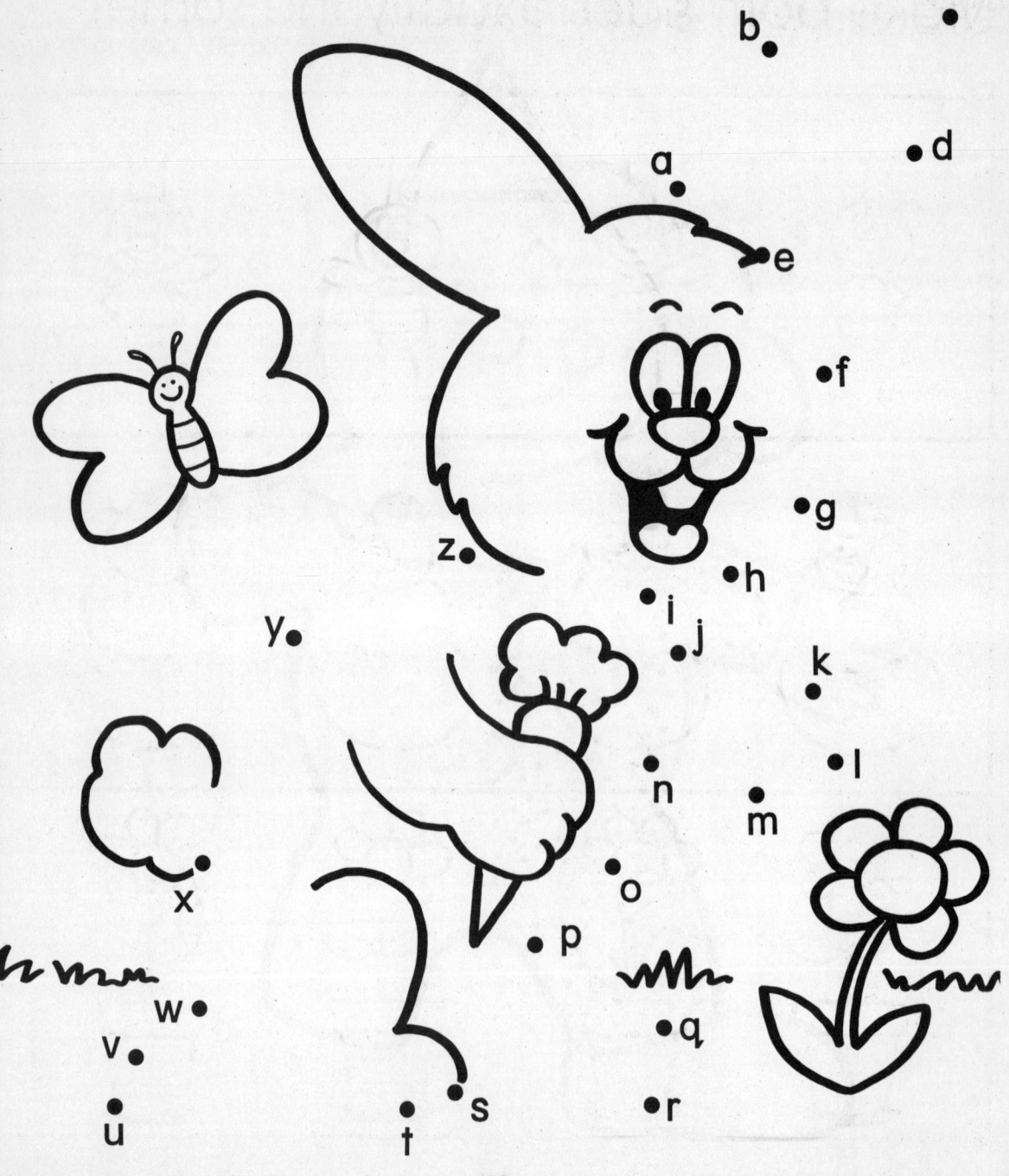

Matching Pairs

Color the two objects that are alike in each row.

Alphabet Practice

Say the name of the letters.
Practice writing the letters.

Aa Aa Bb

Cc Dd

Ee Ff

Gg Hh

Ii Jj

Kk Ll

Mm	Nn
Oo	Pp
Qq	Rr
Ss	Tt
Uu	Vv
Ww	Xx
Yy	Zz

Listen to the Starting Sound

Color the pictures that
start with the same sound as 🐝.

Sssssssssss!

Color the pictures that start with the same sound as 🐍.

Cute Cats

Color the pictures that start with the same sound as

Mmmmmmmm!

Color the pictures that start with the same sound as 🐭.

A Beautiful Butterfly

Color the butterfly.
Make both wings the same.

ABC Order

Connect the dots from **A** to **Z**.

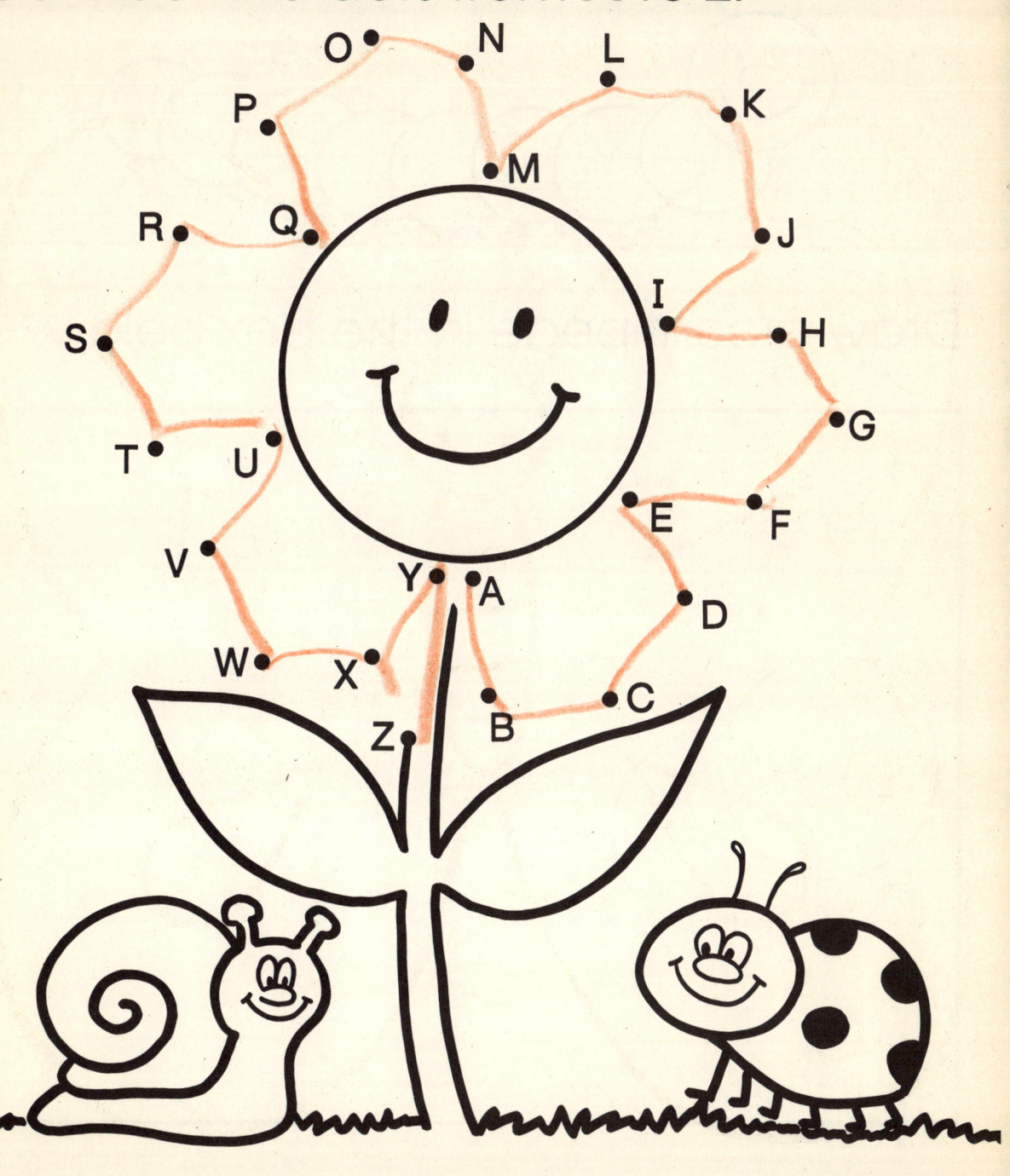

Silly Centipede

Draw a centipede in the box below.

Count The Pictures

Circle the correct number in each box.

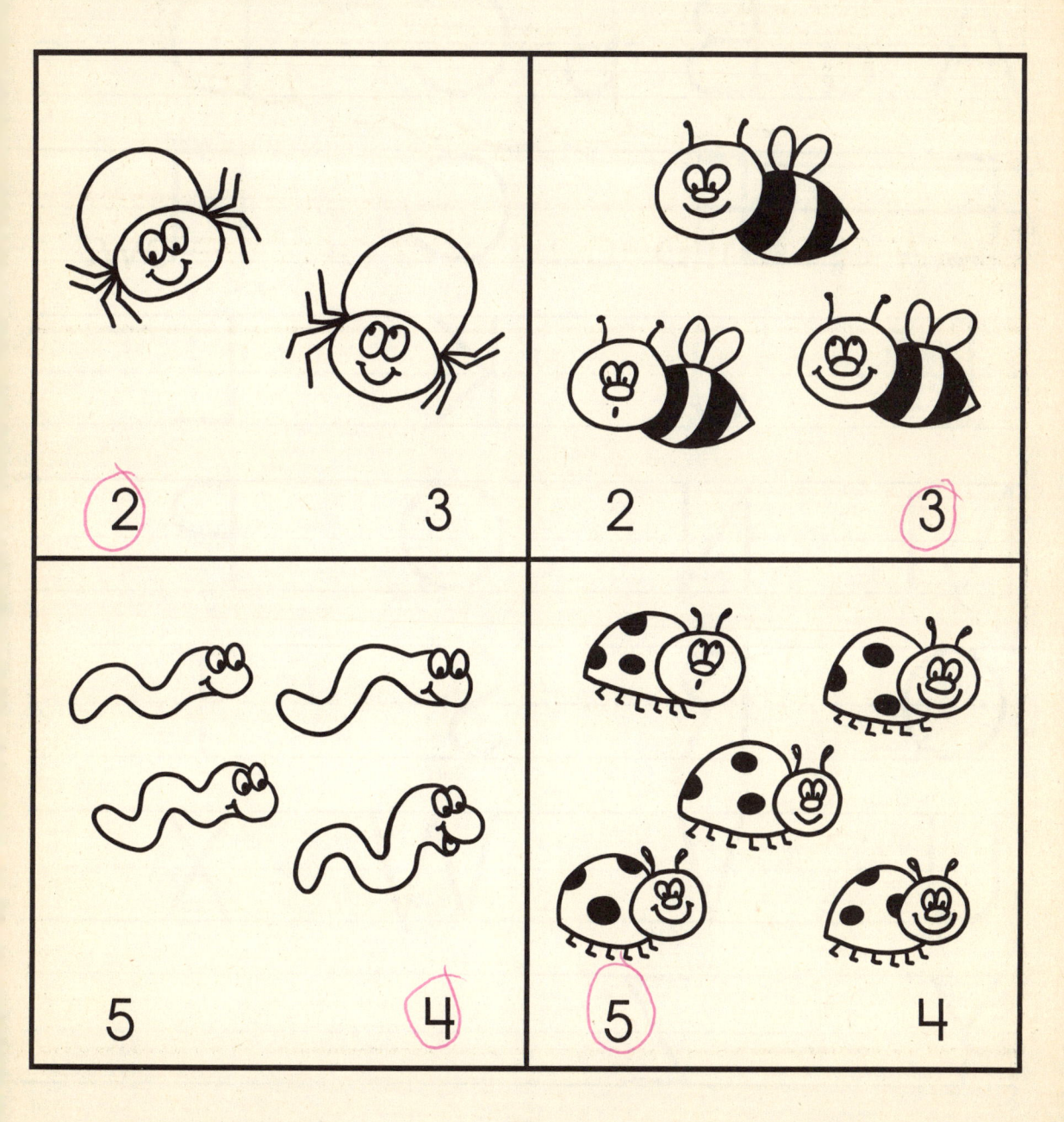

(2) 3	2 (3)
5 (4)	(5) 4

51

Two Kinds of Letters!

Write the lowercase letters.

A a B b C D

E F G H

I J K L

M N O P

Q R S T

U V W X

Y Z